D0108409

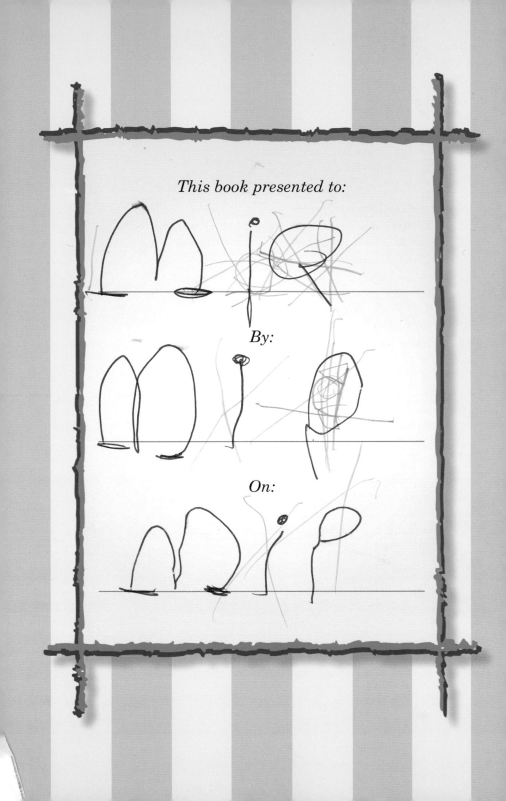

This book presented to:

By:

On:

To the Adult:

Early readers need two kinds of reading. They need to be read to, and they need to do their own reading. *The Hear Me Read Bible* helps you to encourage your child with both kinds.

For example, your child might read this book as you sit together. Listen attentively. Assist gently, if needed. Encourage, be patient, and be very positive about your child's efforts.

Then perhaps you'd like to share the selected Bible story in an easy-to-understand translation. At the beginning of each story in *The Hear Me Read Bible*, we've added a few words of encouragement to aid you in teaching Bible concepts to your little one.

Using both types of reading gives your child a chance to develop new skills and confidence in reading. You share and support your child's excitement.

As a mother and a teacher, I anticipate the joy your child will feel in saying, "Hear me read Bible stories!"

Mary Manz Simon

The Hear·Me·Read BiBLe

By Dr. Mary Manz Simon

Illustrated by Dennis Jones

CONCORDIA PUBLISHING HOUSE • SAINT LOUIS

For Eldon Meyer,
my favorite Road Warrior.

Philippians 1:3

Copyright © 2010 Concordia Publishing House
3558 S. Jefferson Avenue, St. Louis, MO 63118-3968
1-800-325-3040 · www.cph.org

All rights reserved. Unless specifically noted, no part of this publication may be reproduced, stored in a retrieval system, or transmitted, in any form or by any means, electronic, mechanical, photocopying, recording, or otherwise, without the prior written permission of Concordia Publishing House.

Written by Mary Manz Simon

Text copyright © 1990, 1991, 1992, 2010 Concordia Publishing House

Illustrations copyright © Concordia Publishing House

Unless otherwise indicated, Scripture quotations from the ESV Bible® (The Holy Bible, English Standard Version®), copyright © 2001 by Crossway Bibles, a publishing ministry of Good News Publishers. Used by permission. All rights reserved.

Scripture quotations marked NIV are taken from the HOLY BIBLE, NEW INTERNATIONAL VERSION®. NIV®. Copyright © 1973, 1978, 1984 by International Bible Society. Used by permission of Zondervan Publishing House. All rights reserved.

Manufactured in China.   HeShan, China/047365/300306

2   3   4   5   6   7   8   9   10   19   18   17   16   15   14   13   12

TABLE OF CONTENTS

Accelerated Reader
ENTERPRISE

To find the Accelerated Reader tests for these titles, go to the Accelerated Reader™ online catalog at www.arbookfind.com, select "parent" or "teacher," and enter "Simon, Mary Manz" or "Hear Me Read" in the Quick Search window.

What Next?

Genesis 1–2 (Creation)

Young children have a close-up view of God's creation. That's true not because children are short, but because they see the world so clearly. A child marvels at an ant carrying a heavy load, while we reach for the bug spray. On a cold winter day, a child catches a snowflake on his mitten, while we lean heavily on the shovel. But our life experiences and adult cynicism can be stripped away, if only for a moment, when we see the wonders of God's creation through the eyes of a child.

Word List

- ❏ is
- ❏ God
- ❏ see
- ❏ day
- ❏ good
- ❏ look
- ❏ made

- ❏ make
- ❏ next
- ❏ this
- ❏ what
- ❏ will
- ❏ happen

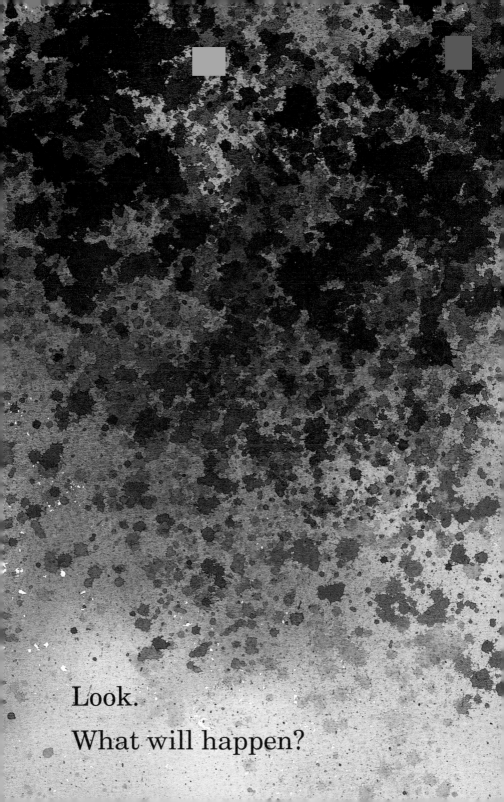

Look.

What will happen?

See what God made.

This is good.

This is day 1.

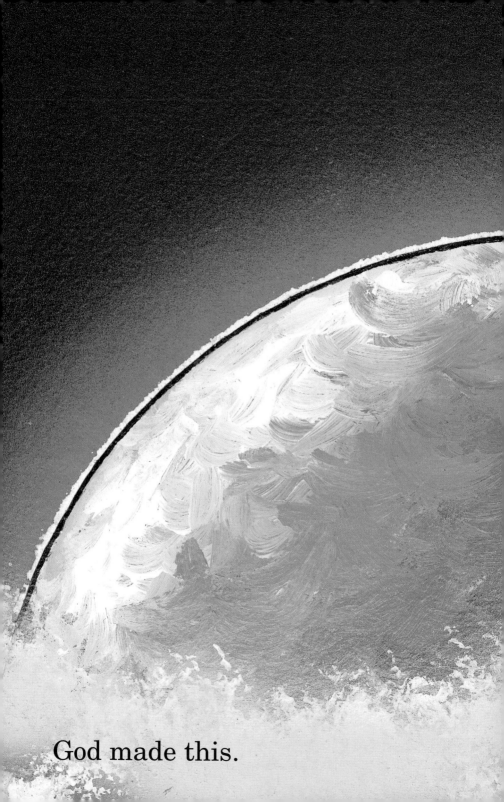

God made this.

This is good.

This is day 2.

What will happen next?

See what God made.

This is good.

This is day 3.

What will happen next?

Look.

God made this.

This is good.

This is day 4.

What will happen next?

See what God made.

This is good.

This is day 5.

What will happen next?

Look.

God made this.

This is good.

This is day 6.

See what God made.

This is day 7.

This is good.

This is good.

Drip Drop

Genesis 6–8 (Noah's Ark)

T he numbers associated with this story are mind-boggling: Noah was 600 years old when the flood began. The ark was as tall as a four- or five-story building. It rained for forty days and forty nights. Although the numbers impress us, they probably will not impress your child. Instead, your child might ask questions like, "Did Noah take a garter snake and a cobra on the ark? Did the elephants sleep standing up?" Such questions obviously do not reflect the key point in the story, that Noah obeyed God. But a child's questions can not only begin a conversation of significance, but also offer insights about a child's level of understanding.

Word List

- ❏ a
- ❏ I
- ❏ at
- ❏ to
- ❏ big
- ❏ God
- ❏ the
- ❏ was
- ❏ boat
- ❏ drip
- ❏ drop
- ❏ God's
- ❏ look
- ❏ make
- ❏ Noah
- ❏ rain
- ❏ said
- ❏ send
- ❏ such
- ❏ will
- ❏ hurry
- ❏ never
- ❏ helper
- ❏ splash
- ❏ promise

Look at Noah.

Noah was God's helper.

God said to Noah,
"Make a boat.
Make a big boat."

"I promise I will send
a big rain," said God.
Hurry, Noah! Hurry!

Drip, drop.

Hurry, Noah! Hurry!

Make a big boat.

Drip, drop.

Drip, drop.

Drip, drop, splash!

Noah was God's helper.

Drip, drop.

Drip, drop.

Drip, drop, splash!

Look at Noah make a boat.

Look at Noah make a big boat.

Drip, drop.

Drip, drop.

Drip, drop, splash!

Hurry, Noah! Hurry!

Splash, splash!

"Look at the big boat.

Look at the big rain.

God said, "I promise I will
never send
such a big rain."

"Look," said Noah.

"Look at God's promise."

Jibber Jabber

Genesis: 11:1–9 (The Tower of Babel)

An infant babbles, but toddlers and preschoolers often "jibber jabber" when they put together meaningless syllables as they experiment with various combinations of sounds. Conversations among the men of Babel might have sounded like the babbling of a baby or toddler. To give your child a different perspective of this Bible story, speak to your child in another language or put together nonsense words. This is an ideal time to remind your child that God understands the prayers of everyone, regardless of the language.

Word List

- ❏ is
- ❏ at
- ❏ is
- ❏ up
- ❏ we
- ❏ are
- ❏ did
- ❏ God
- ❏ mixed
- ❏ tower
- ❏ forgot
- ❏ people
- ❏ not
- ❏ the
- ❏ bake
- ❏ great
- ❏ make
- ❏ said
- ❏ what
- ❏ brick
- ❏ will
- ❏ build
- ❏ look(ed)
- ❏ jibber-jabber

"We are great," said the people.

"We are great people."

"We will build a tower.
We will build a great tower."

"People will look at the tower.
People will say we are great."

Make a brick.

Bake a brick.

Build a tower.

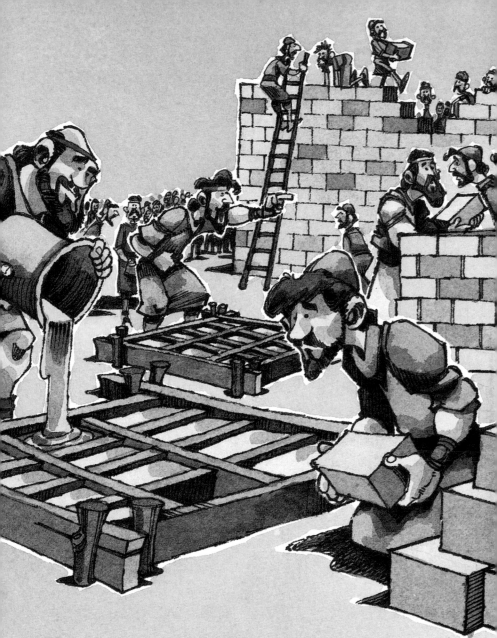

The people looked at the tower.

What a tower!

Up! Up!

Make a brick.

Bake a brick.

Build a tower.

The people looked at the tower.

What a tower!

Up! Up! Up!

Make a brick.

Bake a brick.

Build a tower.

The people looked at the tower.

What a tower!

Up! Up! Up! Up!

God looked at the tower.

God looked at the people.

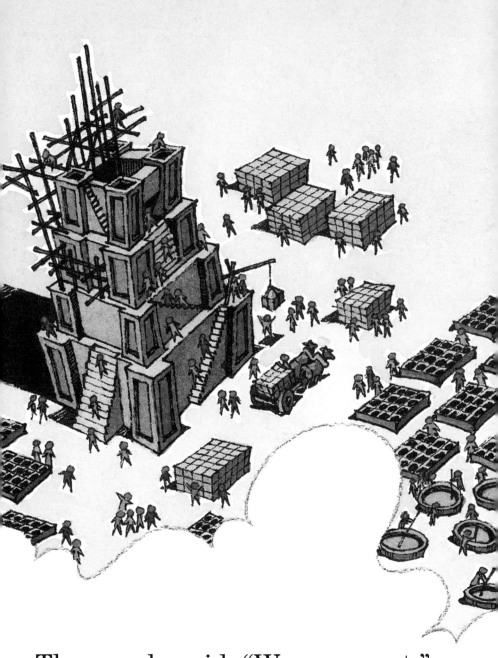

The people said, "We are great."

The people forgot, "God is great."

God mixed up
what the people said.

"Jibber-jabber," said the people.

"Jibber-jabber, jibber-jabber,"
said the people.

The people did not say,

"We are great."

God is great.

Hide the Baby

Exodus 2:1–10 (The Birth of Moses)

H ide the Baby" has elements that make this a beloved Bible story: a baby, soldiers, a princess, intrigue, and a happy ending. A young child might think, "That's a nice story." And it is. Years from now, your child will understand that this story of the baby in a basket is part of God's incredible plan for Moses and the Hebrew people. Sharing this story early in your child's life provides a building block for future spiritual growth.

Word List

- ❑ a
- ❑ of
- ❑ oh
- ❑ are
- ❑ God
- ❑ the
- ❑ you
- ❑ baby

- ❑ care
- ❑ hide
- ❑ hush
- ❑ take
- ❑ will
- ❑ sleep
- ❑ coming
- ❑ soldiers

Oh, a baby.

Hush, baby, hush.

Sleep, baby, sleep.
God will take care of you.

Oh, soldiers are coming.

The soldiers are coming!

Hide the baby.

Hush, baby, hush.

Sleep, baby, sleep.

God will take care of you.

Oh, the soldiers are coming.

The soldiers are coming!

Hide the baby.

Hush, baby, hush.

Sleep, baby, sleep.

God will take care of you.

Oh, a baby.

Hush, baby, hush.

Hush, baby, hush.

Will you take care of the baby?

Hush, baby, hush.

Sleep, baby, sleep.

God will take care of you.

Toot! Toot!

Joshua 5:13–6:20 (The Fall of Jericho)

My dad is bigger than your dad." That reflection of one-up-manship echoes in playgroups and playgrounds. The story of Joshua at Jericho presents the ultimate statement for not merely a childish game, but for life itself. "My God can do anything." God can. That's a fact. God can help us be more patient. God can help us become a more effective parent. God can give us a sense of peace at the end of a hectic day. As your child is reminded in this story, God is all-powerful. That was true long ago when Joshua lived, and it's true today. God can _____. Just fill in the blank!

Word List

- ❑ in
- ❑ to
- ❑ get
- ❑ the
- ❑ can
- ❑ how
- ❑ has
- ❑ and
- ❑ God
- ❑ had
- ❑ was
- ❑ big
- ❑ toot
- ❑ fell
- ❑ walls
- ❑ gates
- ❑ said
- ❑ again
- ❑ march
- ❑ around
- ❑ people
- ❑ praise
- ❑ Jericho
- ❑ Joshua
- ❑ trumpets

Jericho was big.

Jericho had big walls.

Jericho had big gates.

Jericho was big.

Joshua said to God,

"How can the people get in?

Jericho has big walls.

Jericho has big gates."

God said to Joshua,

"The people can get in."

"March around Jericho.

March around the big walls.

March around the big gates.

Toot the trumpets," said God.

March 2–3–4.

March 2–3–4.

Toot!

Toot!

"How can the people get in?"

Joshua said to God.

God said to Joshua,

"March around Jericho again.

March around the big walls again.

March around the big gates again.

Toot the trumpets again."

March 2–3–4.

March 2–3–4.

Toot!

Toot!

"Again," said God.

"March and toot.

March and toot."

"Again," said God.

"Again," said God.

March 2–3–4.

March 2–3–4.

Toot! Toot!

The walls fell.

The gates fell.

Jericho fell.

Toot!

Toot!

Praise God!

Bing!

1 Samuel 17:1–52 (David and Goliath)

Although the story of David and Goliath is often included on a child's list of favorites, the death of Goliath can create challenges for a parent who tries to teach non-violent problem solving. After all, we teach our children not to hit. "Be nice," we encourage, and yet in this story, David kills Goliath. As you and your child discuss the story, focus on other important facts your child can learn: David was brave. David trusted God. God helped David.

Word List

- ❑ a
- ❑ I
- ❑ me
- ❑ at
- ❑ no
- ❑ had
- ❑ was
- ❑ big
- ❑ the
- ❑ who
- ❑ God
- ❑ bing
- ❑ Goliath
- ❑ said
- ❑ help(ed)
- ❑ little
- ❑ fight
- ❑ David
- ❑ sword
- ❑ armor
- ❑ helmet
- ❑ teased
- ❑ looked
- ❑ will
- ❑ soldier(s)

Goliath was a big soldier.

Goliath had armor.

Goliath had a helmet.

Goliath had a sword.

Goliath teased the soldiers.

"Who will fight me?"

Goliath teased.

The soldiers looked at Goliath.
The soldiers looked at the armor.

"Who will fight me?"

Goliath teased.

The soldiers looked at the helmet.

The soldiers looked at the sword.

"No," said the soldiers.

"Who will fight Goliath?"

"I will fight Goliath," said David.

The soldiers looked at David.

David was little.

The soldiers looked at Goliath.

Goliath was big.

Goliath had armor.

Goliath had a helmet.

Goliath had a sword.

"I will fight Goliath,"
said David.
"God will help me."

"I will help," said the soldier.

The soldier had armor.

The soldier had a helmet.

The soldier had a sword.

"No," said David.

"God will help me.

God will help me fight Goliath."

Goliath looked at little David.

David looked at big Goliath.

David looked at the armor.

David looked at the helmet.

David looked at the sword.

"God helped me," said David.

"God helped me fight Goliath."

Whoops!

Jonah 1, 2, 3:1–3 (Jonah and the Fish)

Jonah is often included on a child's list of favorite Bible stories. Yet a five-year-old rarely considers what a yucky, stinky, slimy experience Jonah might have had in the belly of the big fish. But that's not the point of the story. The takeaway should be "obey God." When we follow God's rules, we stay safe and keep out of trouble. That's the underlying lesson in this story—a lesson worth learning at any age!

Word List

- ❏ I
- ❏ am
- ❏ do
- ❏ go
- ❏ me
- ❏ to
- ❏ did
- ❏ God
- ❏ the
- ❏ not
- ❏ now
- ❏ city

- ❏ said
- ❏ tell
- ❏ want(ed)
- ❏ will
- ❏ away
- ❏ from
- ❏ about
- ❏ Jonah
- ❏ people
- ❏ sorry
- ❏ whoops

"Go," said God.

"Go to the city.

Go to the city now."

"Tell the people about Me," said God.
"Tell the people I am God."

"I do not want to go," said Jonah.
"I do not want to go to the city."

"I will not go to the city," said Jonah.

"I will not go to the city now."

"I will go away from God,"
said Jonah.

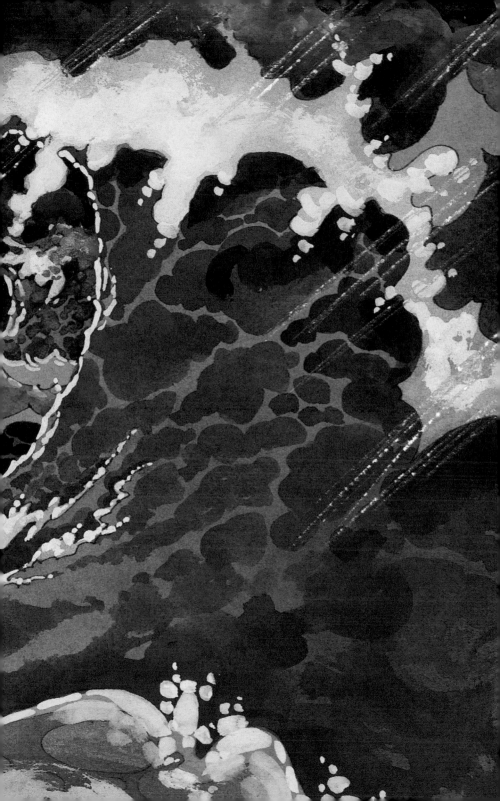

Whoops!

"I did not want to go to the city,"
said Jonah.
"I wanted to go away from God."

"Now I am sorry," said Jonah.
"I am sorry I wanted to
go away from God.
I am sorry I did not
go to the city."

Whoops!

"Go," said God.

"Go to the city.

Go to the city now."

"Tell the people about Me," God said.

"Tell the people I am God."

"I will go," said Jonah.

"I will go now."

"I will go to the city," said Jonah.
"I will tell the people about God."

Send a Baby

Luke 1:5–25; 57–64
(The Birth of John the Baptist)

Like many couples, Elizabeth and Zechariah had spent years praying for the gift of a child. When their son, John, was finally born, he was welcomed into a family that loved him. Use this Bible story as an opportunity to talk with your child about his babyhood. Look at the photos or videos. Compare his baby shoes with the shoes he wears today. Let him snuggle in his baby blanket. As you recall the birth experience, you will both be reminded of the incredible blessing of a child.

Word List

- ❑ a
- ❑ I
- ❑ an
- ❑ do
- ❑ oh
- ❑ to
- ❑ and
- ❑ for
- ❑ God('s)
- ❑ not
- ❑ you
- ❑ baby
- ❑ John
- ❑ said
- ❑ send
- ❑ sent
- ❑ talk
- ❑ then
- ❑ want
- ❑ will
- ❑ angel
- ❑ prayed
- ❑ believe
- ❑ Elizabeth
- ❑ Zechariah

"I want a baby,"

said Elizabeth.

"I want a baby,"

said Zechariah.

Elizabeth and Zechariah
prayed to God.
Elizabeth and Zechariah
prayed to God for a baby.

"I want a baby,"
said Elizabeth.

"I want a baby,"
said Zechariah.

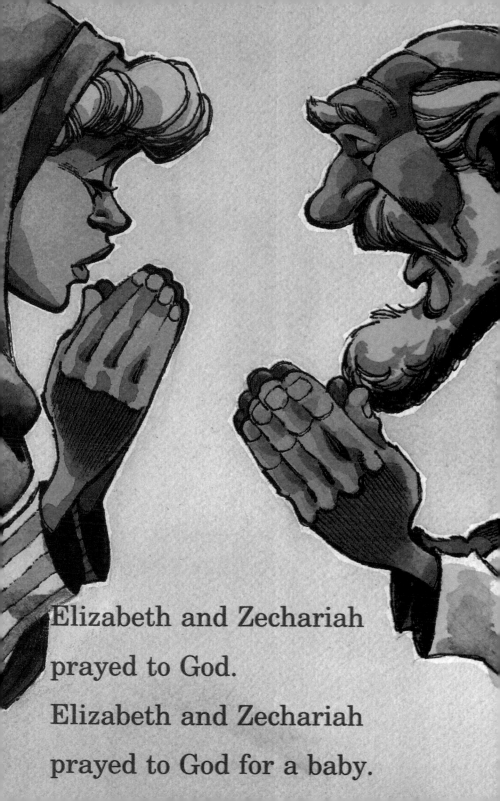

Elizabeth and Zechariah
prayed to God.
Elizabeth and Zechariah
prayed to God for a baby.

Will God send a baby?

Elizabeth and Zechariah

prayed and prayed.

Will God send a baby?

God sent an angel.

God's angel said,

"God will send a baby.

God will send baby John."

Zechariah said, "Oh?"

God's angel said,

"You do not believe God.
You will not talk."

"God will send a baby.

God will send baby John.

Then you will talk."

God sent a baby.

God sent baby John.

Zechariah talked.

Zechariah said,

"I believe God.

I do believe God.

"God sent a baby.

God sent baby John."

A Silent Night

Luke 2:8–20 (Christmas)

A young child often demonstrates sounds made by animals in the Bethlehem stable as he re-arranges the various crèche figures beneath a Christmas tree, so few children would describe the first Christmas as a silent night. But whether or not it was noisy in the stable, holiday distractions can easily drown out the meaning of Jesus' birth. Only the message of the angels cuts through the clutter: Jesus is born. Jesus is born for you!

Word List

- a
- at
- is
- go
- baa
- coo
- the
- look
- said
- born

- night
- sheep
- birds
- Jesus
- angel
- silent
- donkey
- shepherd
- hee-haw
- holy

"Baa, baa," said the sheep.

"Coo, coo," said the birds.

"Hee-haw," said the donkey.

"Baa," said the sheep.

"Coo," said the birds.

"Hee-haw," said the donkey.

A silent night, a holy night.

Look! Look!

"Jesus is born!"
said the angel.

"Jesus is born!"

"Go," said the angel.

"Go look at Jesus."

"Baa, baa," said the sheep.

"Coo, coo," said the birds.

"Hee-haw," said the donkey.

A silent night.

A holy night.

"Jesus?" said the shepherd.

"Jesus.

Look at Jesus."

"Jesus!" said the shepherd.

"Jesus is born."

"Baa, baa," said the sheep.

"Coo, coo," said the birds.

"Hee-haw," said the donkey.

"Jesus is born,"

said the shepherd.

A silent night, a holy night.

Jesus is born.

Follow That Star

Matthew 2:1–11 (The Wise Men)

The journey of the Magi provides a dramatic conclusion to the Christmas story. If weather permits, read the story outdoors at night. Or use a flashlight to read the text, then shine the light on the ceiling after reading the last page. Adding such simple, dramatic touches to Bible stories often triggers conversation about the story. Encourage your child to talk about what he's just read. Or ask questions that will help him think beyond the pages of this book. For example, "What would be fun about riding a camel? What would be hard? What gift would you give to Jesus?"

Word List

- ❏ at
- ❏ is
- ❏ to
- ❏ for
- ❏ see
- ❏ bump
- ❏ let's
- ❏ look
- ❏ rode
- ❏ star
- ❏ that
- ❏ they
- ❏ Jesus
- ❏ where
- ❏ follow
- ❏ bumpety
- ❏ sparkle

Look.

See that star?

See that star sparkle?

That star is for Jesus.

Let's follow that star.

Let's see Jesus.

Bumpety bump.

Bumpety bump they rode.

Where is Jesus?

See that star?

See the star sparkle?

Follow that star.

Bumpety bump.

Bumpety bump they rode.

That star is for Jesus.

Let's follow that star.

Bumpety bump.

Bumpety bump they rode.

They rode to see Jesus.

That star!

That star!

Where is Jesus?

They see Jesus.

Look at Jesus!

Rumble, Rumble

Mark 6:32–44 (Jesus Feeds the Crowd)

A young child does not understand concepts of time and space. That's why the number of people in this story is insignificant to a five or six year old. All he needs to know is that Jesus provided food for a lot of hungry people. When sharing a Bible story, it's easy to get so caught up in making sure a child knows the facts that we miss the biblical teaching. A child should come away from this story knowing that God provides what we need. That's the bottom line. We might be surprised at how He does that or wonder at His timing, but we can be confident that just as God cared for people long ago, He cares for us today.

Word List

- ☐ is
- ☐ to
- ☐ we
- ☐ are
- ☐ for
- ☐ say
- ☐ the
- ☐ you
- ☐ food
- ☐ here
- ☐ may
- ☐ said
- ☐ some
- ☐ want
- ☐ Jesus
- ☐ thank
- ☐ hungry
- ☐ listen
- ☐ people
- ☐ rumble
- ☐ getting
- ☐ grumble
- ☐ stomachs

Here are many people.

Here is Jesus.

The people listen to Jesus.

Many people listen to Jesus.

The people are getting hungry.

Rumble, rumble;
stomachs grumble.

"We are hungry," the people say.

Rumble, rumble;
stomachs grumble.

Jesus said,

"The people want some food."

"Here is some food,"
the people say.

"Here are many, many people,"
said Jesus.

Rumble, rumble;
stomachs grumble.

Jesus said, "Here is some food."

"Here is some food,"
said the people.

"Thank you for the food,"
said the people.

Many, many people
said thank you to Jesus.

Who Will Help?

Luke 10:25–37 (The Good Samaritan)

We assume that because we say, "Be kind to your brother," a young child knows what kindness is. But a young child truly understands the definition only when the word is linked to a compassionate action. That's why we *show* what the word means: we put a Band-Aid on a skinned knee. The meaning of compassion makes the most sense to a child when he not only observes our kind acts, but when he is kind. When we say, "Let's help our neighbor rake the lawn," a child practices the same kind of caring from the heart shown by the Good Samaritan.

Word List

- ☐ a
- ☐ I
- ☐ be
- ☐ he
- ☐ no
- ☐ oh
- ☐ man
- ☐ the
- ☐ who
- ☐ back
- ☐ come
- ☐ down
- ☐ help
- ☐ road
- ☐ said
- ☐ soon
- ☐ walk
- ☐ will
- ☐ cannot
- ☐ walked
- ☐ good-bye

"Good-bye," said the man.

"I will come back soon."

Walk, walk, walk.

The man walked down the road.

"Oh," said the man.

"Oh, no!" said the man.

"Oh, no!" he said.

"Who will help?"

"I cannot walk.

I cannot walk down the road."

Walk, walk, walk.

A man walked down the road.

"Help!" said the man.

"Come help."

"I cannot help," he said.

He walked down the road.

"Oh, no!" said the man.

"Who will help?"

Walk, walk, walk.

A man walked down the road.

"Help!" said the man.

"Come help."

"I cannot help," he said.

He walked down the road.

"Oh, no!" said the man.

"Who will help?"

Walk, walk, walk.

A man walked down the road.

"Help!" said the man.

"Come help."

"I will help," he said.

Walk, walk, walk.
Walk down the road.

"Good-bye," said the man.

"I will be back soon."

Sit Down!

Luke 10:38–42 (Mary and Martha)

Mary and Martha scurried around to prepare an adequate welcome for Jesus. And yet when their Guest arrived, Mary re-ordered her priorities: she put "learn from Jesus" at the top of her list. She might have noticed a dust bunny in the kitchen corner, but she stopped to sit at the feet of Jesus. Prioritizing our own spiritual growth or nurturing a child to grow up with Jesus can easily slide down on our list of priorities ... after all, there are so many things to do. Yet if we're honest with ourselves, we will admit that the Mary in this story got it right.

Word List

- ❏ to
- ❏ and
- ❏ not
- ❏ sat
- ❏ sit
- ❏ yum
- ❏ come
- ❏ down
- ❏ here
- ❏ Mary
- ❏ said
- ❏ will
- ❏ Jesus
- ❏ swept
- ❏ swish
- ❏ cooked
- ❏ Martha
- ❏ work(ed)
- ❏ listened

Mary swept. Swish, swish, swish.
Martha cooked. Yum, yum, yum.
Mary and Martha worked,
worked, worked.

"Jesus will come," said Mary.

"Jesus will come here,"
said Martha.

Mary swept. Swish, swish, swish.

Martha cooked. Yum, yum, yum.

Mary and Martha worked.

"Come," said Mary.

"Jesus, Jesus," said Martha.

"Come," said Mary.

"Come and sit down.

Come and sit down here."

Jesus sat down.

Mary sat down.

Mary listened to Jesus.

Martha swept.

Swish, swish, swish.

Martha worked, worked, worked.

Mary listened to Jesus.

Martha cooked. Yum, yum, yum.
Martha worked, worked, worked.

Mary listened to Jesus.

Martha worked, worked, worked.

Martha sat down.

Mary listened to Jesus.

Martha said,

"Mary will not work.

Mary will not come and work."

Jesus said, "Come here, Martha.
Come and sit down."

Martha sat down.

Martha listened to Jesus.

Mary and Martha
listened to Jesus.

Come to Jesus

Mark 10:13–16
(Jesus Blesses the Children)

A young child experiences the love of Jesus through us. That can be a disturbing thought, especially after we respond to a situation out of anger, frustration, or impatience. And yet it's true: a child experiences the love of Jesus through us. It is also true that when we open our hearts to God's gifts of grace and forgiveness, we experience the love of Jesus.

Word List

- ❏ go(ing)
- ❏ no
- ❏ to
- ❏ us
- ❏ see
- ❏ the
- ❏ call(s)
- ❏ will
- ❏ with
- ❏ bless
- ❏ come
- ❏ we're
- ❏ child
- ❏ Jesus
- ❏ cannot
- ❏ hooray
- ❏ people
- ❏ children

1, 2.

2 people.

2 people go to see Jesus.

The child calls,

"We're going to see Jesus.
Hooray! Hooray!"

"Come.

Come with us.

Come with us to see Jesus."

1, 2, 3, 4, 5.

5 people.

5 people go to see Jesus.

The children call,

"We're going to see Jesus."

"Come.

Come with us.

Come with us to see Jesus."

1, 2, 3, 4, 5, 6, 7.

7 people.

7 people go to see Jesus.

The children call,

"We're going to see Jesus.

Hooray! Hooray!"

"Come.

Come with us.

Come with us to see Jesus."

1, 2, 3, 4, 5, 6, 7, 8, 9, 10.

10 people.

10 people go to see Jesus.

The children call,

"We're going to see Jesus.

Hooray! Hooray!"

"Children, see Jesus?

See Jesus?"

"Come.
Come with us.
Jesus will bless the children."

"No.

The children cannot come.

The children cannot
come to see Jesus."

"Come."

Too Tall, Too Small

Luke 19:1–10 (Zacchaeus)

The story of Zacchaeus offers an ideal opportunity to help a child compare and contrast height. However, this "wee little man" is only the starting point: use your child as the central figure in this word game. Ask, "Who's taller than you? Shorter? The same height?" Maintain a playful tone by inserting some suggestions a young child might think are silly, for example, "Are you taller than a giraffe? Are you shorter than a mouse?" To answer these questions, a child must first visualize the animal, then mentally compare himself. He might need to pause for a moment. That's good: it shows he's practicing mental gymnastics, more commonly called "thinking."

Word List

❏ I	❏ too	❏ trees
❏ to	❏ are	❏ close
❏ am	❏ wow	❏ climb
❏ up	❏ want	❏ small
❏ be	❏ tall	❏ Jesus
❏ me	❏ will	❏ people
❏ see	❏ come	❏ animals
❏ the	❏ said	❏ Zacchaeus

See the people.

The people want to see Jesus.

"I want to see Jesus,"
said Zacchaeus.
"I want to see Jesus, too."

"The people are too tall,"

said Zacchaeus.

"I am too small."

"I will climb up, up to see,"
said Zacchaeus.
"Jesus will be close to me."

"The people are too tall.

The animals are too tall.

I am too small,"

said Zacchaeus.

"I will climb up, up to see,"

said Zacchaeus.

"Jesus will be close to me."

See the people.

See the animals.

See Zacchaeus.

"The people are too tall.

The animals are too tall.

The trees are too tall.

I am too small," said Zacchaeus.

"I want to see Jesus.

"I want to see Jesus, too."

The people are tall.

The animals are tall.

The trees are tall.

"The trees are tall,"
said Zacchaeus.
"Wow!"

"I will climb the trees,"

said Zacchaeus.

"I will climb the tall, tall trees."

"I will climb up, up to see,"
said Zacchaeus.
"Jesus will be close to me."

"I see Jesus.

I see Jesus come.

Jesus will see me,"
    said Zacchaeus.

"Zacchaeus," said Jesus.
"Zacchaeus, come see Me.
Come close to Me."

"Wow!" said Zacchaeus.

Hurry, Hurry!

Matthew 21:1–11
(Jesus Enters Jerusalem)

Children love a parade. Flags, floats, bands, and even (or especially!) the candy tossed by marchers combine to make a memorable day. Help your child capture the excitement of Palm Sunday by acting out the story. Lay towels on the floor. Invite your child to wave his arms and shout, "Hosanna." This "play acting" does not need to be lengthy or fancy. It is easier for a child to remember a Bible story when he is mentally and physically engaged in re-telling that story.

Word List

❏ a
❏ is
❏ to
❏ we
❏ for
❏ run
❏ the
❏ come
❏ let's

❏ must
❏ hurry
❏ Jesus
❏ there
❏ where
❏ parade

Hurry, hurry!

There is a parade.

The parade is for Jesus.

Come to the parade for Jesus.

Hurry, hurry!

We must run to the parade.

Where is the parade?

Where is the parade for Jesus?

Come!

Come to the parade.

Let's run!

Where is the parade?

Where is the parade for Jesus?

Run, run!

Hurry, hurry!

Come to the parade.

There is the parade.

There is Jesus.

Come to Jesus.

Where Is Jesus?

Matthew 27:62–66; 28:1–9 (Easter)

The Easter story is the foundation of the Christian faith, but the events surrounding the resurrection of Jesus can be difficult to communicate to young children. There is darkness, death, and fear. Yet the message of Easter for a child can be summed up in four joyous words: "Come see. Go tell." And so we say to a child, "Look at the empty tomb. Let's tell everyone that Jesus is alive. He is with us every day."

Word List

- ❏ I
- ❏ am
- ❏ be
- ❏ do
- ❏ go
- ❏ in
- ❏ is
- ❏ say
- ❏ the
- ❏ not
- ❏ here
- ❏ rise
- ❏ roll
- ❏ said
- ❏ shut
- ❏ tomb
- ❏ will
- ❏ alive
- ❏ Jesus
- ❏ stone
- ❏ where
- ❏ afraid
- ❏ people

"Jesus is not alive.
Jesus is in the tomb."

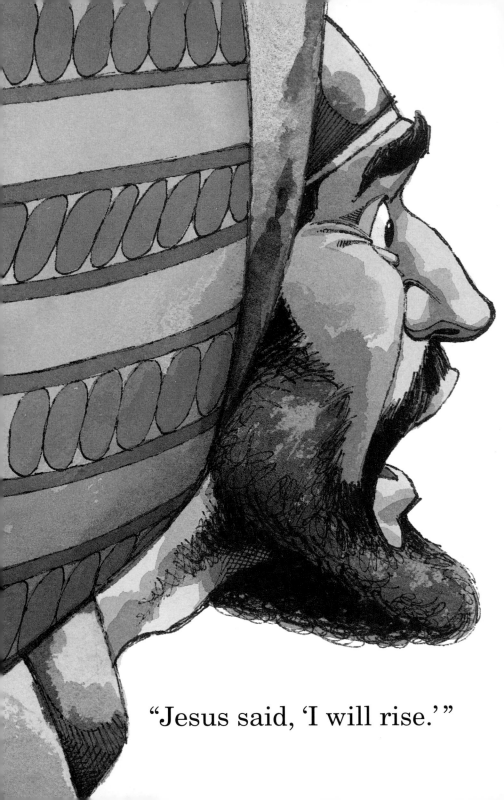

"Jesus said, 'I will rise.'"

"People will say,

'Where is Jesus?'"

"Go!

Shut the tomb."

"Roll, roll the stone."

"Roll the stone here."

The tomb is shut.

"I am not afraid.

The tomb is shut.

People will not say,

'Where is Jesus?' "

"I am not afraid.

Jesus is not alive.

Jesus is in the tomb."

The stone!

The stone!

"Do not be afraid."

"Where is Jesus?"

"Jesus said, 'I will rise.'
Jesus is not here."

"Jesus is alive."

"Go.

Say, 'Jesus is alive!'"

Jesus is alive!

Row the Boat

John 21:1–11 (Jesus Fills the Nets)

Thanks to the familiarity of the nursery song, Row, Row, Row the Boat, even very young children can identify with this story title. Linking a biblical personality, value, or theme to a child's everyday experiences helps the child make a mental connection to the story. You might sing and act out rowing a boat before/after reading Row the Boat. Or you might talk about the boats a child floats in the bathtub. Making these connections is an example of how you can help a child's brain grow.

Word List

- ❑ at
- ❑ no
- ❑ go
- ❑ in
- ❑ are
- ❑ put
- ❑ row
- ❑ man
- ❑ the
- ❑ net

- ❑ let's
- ❑ said
- ❑ boat
- ❑ fish
- ❑ here
- ❑ down
- ❑ look
- ❑ Jesus
- ❑ there
- ❑ fishing

"Let's go fishing," said the man.

"Let's row the boat,"
said the man.

Row, row, row the boat.

"Let's fish here," said the man.

"Put the net down.

Put the net down here."

"No fish!" said the man.
"Look. There are no fish.
There are no fish in the net."

Row, row, row the boat.

"Let's fish here," said the man.

"Put the net down.

Put the net down here."

"No fish!" said the man.

"Look.

There are no fish.

There are no fish in the net."

"Look," said the man.

"Look at the fish."

Row, row, row the boat.

"Put the net down," said the man.

"Put the net down here."

"No fish!" said the man.

"Look.

There are no fish.

There are no fish in the net."

Jesus said, "Go fishing here."

Row, row, row the boat.

Jesus said, "Put the net down."

"Put the net down here."

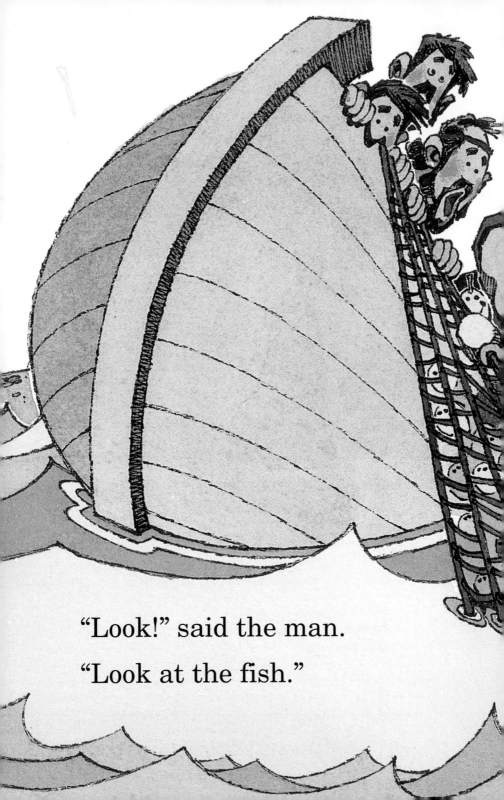

"Look!" said the man.

"Look at the fish."